On the Road Home

Travel Poems

On the Road Home

*Travel Poems
by Joanne Blakley*

CHAPLAIN PUBLISHING
105 S. John Street
Jonesboro, Illinois 62952

Copyright © 2008 by Joanne Blakley

All rights reserved, including the right of reproduction in whole or in part in any form.

Cover Design By: Amanda Urbanski

ISBN 10: 0-9821079-2-7
ISBN 13: 978-0-9821079-2-8

Printed in Nashville, Tennessee
United States of America

CHAPLAIN PUBLISHING
www.chaplainpublishing.com

This book is available from bookstores and online or from the publisher.

FIRST EDITION

$7.95 U.S.

Dedication

This book is dedicated with sincere thanks to the following persons, for their patient help and encouragement . . . *On the Road Home*.

Linda Kall
Kathy Cotton
Jim Lambert
Carol Dooley

The Long Branch Poets

Table of Contents

Where My Heart Is	01
Secure	03
Fairland Flea Market	04
Call of the West	05
Cochiti, New Mexico	06
Santa Fe Laundromat	07
God's Paintbrush	08
Colors of Oklahoma	09
The Legend of Davy Getz	10
Haiku	12
Texas Bayou	13
Cottonwoods	14
The Adamant Crow	15
Childhood Home	16
Northern Illinois	17
Glad to see you, Gladstone	18
To Kit Carson, wherever you are	21
Lesson of the Butterfly	22
Genesis One One	23
Sunday's Sermon	24
Cross my Heart	25
Taste of Graham Crackers	26

When I Die	27
Serendipity	28
Morning Prayer	29
Stop	30
The Life of a Cow	31
In an Instant	32
Haiku	33
Frankie	35
The Cross	37
Post-Massage Poem	38
Davoss's Story	39
Davoss's Skin	41
Davoss as Roommate	42
Davoss and I	43
Waiting	44
Dear Willie	45
Ode to Willie	46
Willie Nelson, Continued	47
Prayer for Peace	48
Prayer for Peace, Part Two	49
Fishing on Hot Summer Day	50
July Haiku	51
Lost Joy	52

Ms. Pam's Classroom	54
Stillness Dances	55
Spring Cleaning	56
Night Time Routine	57
Haiku for Politicians	58
Table of Contents	59
Walking Sixth Street	61
Jonesboro Park in August	63
Hotel Maid	65
Long Ago Summers	66
Brazen Bird	67
Cooking Lesson #1	68
Wedding Date	69
Ancient Dwelling	71
Shall I Write This	73
Lost Love	74
Reading Robert Penn Warren	75
Carl and I	76
October Song	77
Brain Fog	78
Shenandoah Splendor	79
Shenandoah Splendor, Part Two	81
The Anna to Santa Fe Trail, A Travel Journal	83

ON THE ROAD HOME

WHERE MY HEART IS

They say home is where the heart is.
Well, I have many homes.
I'm home in fields and woodlands of northern Illinois,
where young girls dreamed and played,
in mild and friendly southern Illinois,
nested in Shawnee's forested hills.

I'm home in New Mexico's sun-kissed landscape,
built with adobe, turquoise, and tile,
in Virginia's Shenandoah Valley,
where family roots run deep and strong
in Lancaster County, Pennsylvania,
waking to simplicity and clip-clopping hoof beats.

I'm home in Tianjin, China,
where savory street smells
encircle a bustling multitude,
in Tirana, Albania, where bonds of compassion
stand tall and proud.

ON THE ROAD HOME

I'm home in Durango, Colorado's mountain
majesties, refreshing, restoring,
body and soul,
in Oklahoma's cinnamon-colored panhandle,
where ranchers tip their hats
with weathered hands,
in Brazos Bayou, Texas,
where God speaks in a whisper
and nature sings loud and clear.

I'm home in places never seen before
 and never seen again.

Home is where I am.

SECURE

I clasp the
turquoise studded cross
swinging chain
of tarnished gray
hanging from
rear-view mirror

I turn a
corner swerve
avoid bumps
and potholes

The cross
in my hand is
secure
I'm reminded
 "As am I."

ON THE ROAD HOME

FAIRLAND FLEA MARKET

miles from home
familiarity lays a
welcome mat
Lassie lunchboxes
Roy Rogers action figures
Aunt Imogene's scrapbook
Grandma's mandolin

may I linger
find one more treasure
seek an unknown
something
plant my presence in
ground of youth
aunt and grandma's
love

ON THE ROAD HOME

CALL OF THE WEST

Hey, old woman,
why do you sit here
dreaming about the West?

eagles soar Oklahoma sky
cowboys and Indians
celebrate tradition
legend lives on

Whoa! Listen carefully
all roads lead home
don't get lost in scenery
call of wild
unbridled adventure

Romancing a
vanishing frontier
part myth part magic
More than meets the eye

COCHITI, NEW MEXICO

Ancient mesas
call me home,
my brothers of red earth,
souls of sibling bonding in
sacred geography

Standing tall
with piercing eye
nodding, knowing, hearing,
kindred drumbeat of
human heart

Ancient mesas
welcome me home
to dance the dance of celebration
We are the victor warriors
with the love, that conquers all

ON THE ROAD HOME

SANTA FE LAUNDROMAT

sun-scorched dirty-clothed man
puts quarters in a game machine
while a straight-bearing black woman
reads a travel log
and two boys with
backward baseball caps,
speak with pinched eyes
mouths pulled

flouncy woman in billowed skirt
hot pink and sunburst yellow
works quickly beside
bent man with sweaty straw hat
and Spanish-speaking children
run under tables

the multi-cultured tapestry
that is Santa Fe

GOD'S PAINTBRUSH

Just how many colors did you create,
Lord?
Is there a number or
is there, as I suspect,
a limitless spectrum of hues, shades, and
tones
painted across a lovingly diverse palette
of lines, patterns, and textures
with the brush of your holy creative
soul?

ON THE ROAD HOME

COLORS OF OKLAHOMA

cinnamon, paprika,
burnt umber, sepia,
sienna, gray, sage,
straw tan, bronze gold,
and bright, bright, blue

ON THE ROAD HOME

THE LEGEND OF DAVY GETZ

Dayton remembers
the death of Davy Getz
thirty nine years old
mind of a child

Captured in a war
he didn't understand
carrying an open rifle
hunting squirrels he said

Tied to a wagon
a rope around his neck
he staggered behind
their procession through the Valley

On a grassy knoll
forced to dig his own grave
elderly parents begging
bystanders pleading
he was shot

ON THE ROAD HOME

General Custer's orders
No exceptions
This is war

"You'll die a bloody death for this!"
an onlooker yelled

Not everyone knows
about the death of Davy Getz
most everyone's heard
of Custer's

ON THE ROAD HOME

HAIKU

*I love the sound
a creek rock makes
as I cross to the other side*

*plaza Santa Fe
sunshine smells like
toasting chile´s*

*weeds waving
in my garden
welcome home*

ON THE ROAD HOME

TEXAS BAYOU

symphony of sounds
just listen
chattering, piping, whistling
chirping, quacking, honking
fluttering, flapping, twittering, trilling
octaves of echoes
reverberating across swales and sloughs
oxbow lakes and marshes

hushed audience of
moss-draped oaks
twisted sycamores and noble
cottonwoods
stand in ovation
while mud-colored alligators
watch with one eye and
a strutting crane
stretches out its neck
stands still
and waits

ON THE ROAD HOME

COTTONWOODS

walking in Texas
sonnet of sun and blue
whispers of Spanish ladies
speaking solidarity
all is well

thick arms draped in spinster shawls
low reaching
wide reaching
curving, intertwining
dancing

their melody is
strength and love

canopy of crackling leaves
khaki moss breath softened
by salted breeze

all heads bow

ON THE ROAD HOME

THE ADAMANT CROW

insistent bird
calls me to stop and look
I see nothing but
stately cottonwoods
huddled in marsh-covered pasture
the only movement
swaying moss-threads
the only sound
that insistent bird

CHILDHOOD HOME

In treasured memory of
those who lived here
and salted the earth

Emotions wave like
golden grasses in November breeze
so beautiful, my Buffalo Creek Valley

Olden days whisper from
the ruins of Wilson's mill

History walks on moccasined feet

ON THE ROAD HOME

NORTHERN ILLINOIS

I'm home   *sitting in sun*
                               deep breath

childhood
peaks behind
clouded memories

                               I'm here
                               writing

warm blanket
sunshine
the moment

                               and love

ON THE ROAD HOME

GLAD TO SEE YOU, GLADSTONE

miles from home
familiar oasis under
high desert sun
population sparse as landscape
windswept and prairie strong

between Clayton and Springer
ninety mile expanse with
no other tonic
for this tired traveler's soul

at mile marker thirty-six
I stop to stretch
communicate with humanity
ask, what's life like

under this massive sapphire sky and
three hundred sixty degrees
of horizon

ON THE ROAD HOME

twenty-five neighbors in
fifteen square miles,
one hundred fifty miles
from Walmart?

beneath such infinite blue,
does your scope match this sphere,
your honesty match this firmament?
can there be any secrets,
can a speck hide from
a God the size of heaven?

welcome back, smiles Thelma
proprietor of Gladstone Mercantile
artist of cowboy cooking
and southwest décor,
stop awhile and linger
experience roots
deep in treasured past

stroll around the ruins
explore the flotsam and jetsam

ON THE ROAD HOME

of prairie winds and desert sun
examine primordial remnants
of long ago ranches
a wagon-rutted trail

feel the same dry sun and
scratching wind
felt centuries before

come play a game of Bingo
we meet here every month
we'll sing Happy Birthday
laugh and joke and eat

you see,
hardship makes us strong and
openness sets us free

thank you, Gladstone
I tip my hat

ON THE ROAD HOME

TO KIT CARSON, WHEREVER YOU ARE

I met your descendent
his wavy red hair and steely blue eyes
said to come from you
he plays your part, you know
re-enacting the legend
living a hero's story

some say you were a scoundrel
cold-hearted, vindictive
but I found this man a gentleman
unassuming, upright
with a simple, honest smile

so I choose to believe the best
you must have been
more good than bad
your word as sure as the sunrise
I saw it in his eyes

LESSON OF THE BUTTERFLY

Oh butterfly with
broken wing
beaten by prairie winds

will you dance in
my cup of flowers
drink sweet nectar
beside my bed?

Will you teach me
how to live
while teaching me
how to die?

ON THE ROAD HOME

GENESIS ONE ONE

ancient love
solemn eagle
lifts and soars
my heart

SUNDAY'S SERMON

genuine   *love*
sincerity   *wins*

perfect   *faith*
grace   *heals*

holy   *hope*
kindness   *conquers*

fervent   *peace*
trust   *lasts*

God's   *joy*
voice   *speaks*

listen

ON THE ROAD HOME

CROSS MY HEART

deft strokes
subtle power
fingertips touch
periphery
head to sternum
side to side
eyes closed
heart lifted
I pray

TASTE OF GRAHAM CRACKERS

takes me away to
childhood road trips
kindergarten snack times
brown squares dipped in
cups of milk
chin dripping
milk puddles

WHEN I DIE

Will I leave here in pain,
spirit-crushed and defeated?
or will I march out victorious,
rejoicing in the goodness of God?

SERENDIPITY

Chance
Fate
Destiny
Karma
Providence
Luck, fortune, coincidence
Accident
Ha Ha
It's all God

MORNING PRAYER

Grant me grace
Guide me in truth
Lead me in love

ON THE ROAD HOME

STOP

*the stress-filled
thoughts listen
leaves shimmer
birds chatter
pull breath into
every cell
dance*

ON THE ROAD HOME

THE LIFE OF A COW

browse nonchalantly
chew contentedly
watch warily
live bovinely

IN AN INSTANT

stiletto-heeled or
soft-stepping
you walk through
life

head-over-heels
body-slam
reality

life changes

ON THE ROAD HOME

HAIKU

*sun rises
through frosted tress
ice sparkles*

*one hundred robins
hopped and sang
in my backyard*

*sunlit hill
dewdrops shimmer
a crystal dance*

*morning wraps me
in a blanket of blue
rose and lavender*

ON THE ROAD HOME

*early spring sunshine
kisses my face
with the breeze*

*Greetings, lone bird
I almost didn't see you
quiet in spring breeze
Do you enjoy the forest
soak in its stillness
as much as I?*

*Said good morning
to the hyacinths
then walked on my way*

*Heaven's bliss
poured out on earth*

ON THE ROAD HOME

FRANKIE

I remember your huskiness
smell of Copenhagen
sweat and steel
the soot on your face
glint in your eye

I remember your muscled arms
wide hands and broad face
the smile that grinned
the smile that loved

I remember you
tender-hearted tough guy
heart of mischief
friend of all

I remember your
suffering, you squeezed my hand
winked your eye
said you were ready

ON THE ROAD HOME

I must now remember
your immortal soul

ON THE ROAD HOME

authority
power
mission **The Cross** *purpose*
disciple's ultimate command
miracle
love
grace
church
obedience
triumph

POST-MASSAGE POEM

I have to write it
release the energy
bursting inside of me,
love and healing
from holiest of spirits

light touch plus
quiet heart equals
power

ON THE ROAD HOME

DAVOSS' S STORY

Police took me from Mama Pat's house
I rode in a police car
They left my wheel chair and my walker
They pick me up and put me in the
police car

They put me in the state hospital
They gave me too much medicine
I had to wear diapers
They feed me and wipe my mouth

I miss my Mama Pat
She not come see me
I pray the Lord
Help my Mama Pat

I stay a long time
I can't walk anymore
I can't move my legs
I miss my Mama Pat

ON THE ROAD HOME

My teacher come see me
She brought me cookies
I love my teacher
She gave me a hug

She went to the courthouse
The judge say I go home with
 my teacher
Praise the Lord
I got a good life now

Mama Pat, be happy for me

ON THE ROAD HOME

DAVOSS' S SKIN

The color of toasted marshmallow
splotched and scarred
pocked and mottled
soft and supple, like
the tanned hide of weathered beast

DAVOSS AS ROOMMATE

3:00 AM

Bang bang clang clang
Make a lot of noise
Bang bang clang clang
Make a lot of noise

(Repeat)

DAVOSS AND I

I see people watching us
black white
brown blonde
disabled competent
serious silly
"Your nose is running,
shall I buy it some shoes?"

WAITING

meaningless wandering
listless thoughts
inhaling exhaling
one foot in front of other
this way that way
back and forth head down
waiting

DEAR WILLIE

May I shake your hand,
  in a brief instant
  repay all the love
  I can compress into a
  heart beat?

May I answer your smile,
  eye to eye, friend to friend,
  soul to soul?

May I tell you this secret, in case
  you don't already know?

In the beginning was the Word and
  the Word is our gift.

And may I whisper in your ear?
  "Jesus is the Word."

Selah

ODE TO WILLIE

With your chiseled Cherokee face
moxie eyes and childish grin
your voice vibrates a universal chord

my soul smiles

braided bandana'd
Grandma's boy to country crooner
red-headed stranger no more

ON THE ROAD HOME

WILLIE NELSON, CONTINUED

hero of honky-tonk
shepherd of song

PRAYER FOR PEACE

I came upon a dozen deer
who stared blank-faced and frozen
I prayed peace to them
but they didn't listen
and leapt white-tailed into
early morning thicket

PRAYER FOR PEACE, PART TWO

will you listen
to me now, lone deer?
morning's field is
still and calm
dewdrops hug the ground

will you listen
hear love's soft
soulful sound

you may as well
receive the prayer
grounded by
grand design

life's dance
won't last for long

FISHING ON HOT SUMMER DAY

where creek curves
and thick tree grows over water
a place to sit cool in shade
swat sticky flies
Grandma chewed Juicy Fruit gum
spit on the worm and
got a bite every time

ON THE ROAD HOME

JULY HAIKU

duckweed
covers Jonesboro pond
shadows dance

dragonflies
circle and soar
spiders float

LOST JOY

she wears a tin roof
gray-hearted lips pursed
hands folded upon themselves
clasping mistaken wrongs

rocking chair
rhythm silhouettes rain
steely-eyed shadow
trapped in self-styled
prison of unforgiveness

offer to help
hand, heart extended
come outdoors,
the sunshine is glorious
amazing, amazing grace

her reply was a slap
how dare anyone imply
anything amiss

ON THE ROAD HOME

pain and dark
are comfortable

I turn
and walk away

MS. PAM'S CLASSROOM

Paper apples hang from ceiling
students drum and rock and hum
strapped in chairs,
diapered, bibbed,
tube-fed

Paper apples red circles
held by invisible string
just in case one of them
notices

STILLNESS DANCES

Suspended moments
when vision is ephemeral
eclipse of time and place
soul and spirit
stillness dances,
and God says
"Ah-ha."

SPRING CLEANING

My newly cleaned closet,
dust-free and clutter-free,
shoes lined in pairs,
clothes sorted neatly-folded,

How life should be,
neat and tidy and clean.
Peace settles in the corners,
and God's love fills every space.

My internal closet
not quite as pleasant to behold
Oh God, I do need you.
Do a spring-cleaning on my soul.

NIGHT TIME ROUTINE

I lay out rows of cards
one up six down
two up five down
and so on until
bottom row seven up

I move the cards, alternating
red and black descending
numerically,
shuffling, repeating
shuffling, repeating

I read and write awhile
stretch and pray
close my eyes and
somewhere in my brain, hear

that jack plays on that queen
that deuce plays on that three

HAIKU FOR POLITICIANS

truth
by definition
Is always true

ON THE ROAD HOME

TABLE OF CONTENTS

Story of my Life
following title page
is list of highlights
main events
in outline form

missing are details

summer morning sun
smell of fresh hay
the book I read
in one sitting

my heart when I held
my first born

hidden between lines
are petty annoyances
deeds best forgotten

ON THE ROAD HOME

*a catalog of chapters
without verse*

ON THE ROAD HOME

WALKING SIXTH STREET

*Morning walk
in Springfield
  heart of
  Illinois
before sounds of
city rush
fill the air*

*stately structures
painted pillars
dated stones*

*this street
strolled for a century
  and decades more*

*by politicians
lawyers lawmen
bankers clerks
window washers*

ON THE ROAD HOME

street sweepers
  young Abe

and wonder-struck
farm girls
  such as I

ON THE ROAD HOME

JONESBORO PARK IN AUGUST

leaf swirls on
invisible thread
spider's silk dangling

hawk dips
below tree line
wide wings flapping

leaf falls
lazy
wavy

butterfly flies
within an inch
of my face
orange-tipped wings
flutter for attention

ON THE ROAD HOME

I turn my head
   and heart
in his direction

listen to the stillness
he left behind

ON THE ROAD HOME

HOTEL MAID

*sitting backdoor
curbside
tan feet
point inward
bare knees
a shelf for
bent elbows*

*her eyes
hold mine
wizened face
squinting as
she inhales*

*cigarette
held comfortably*

*she appraises
my appearance
the anonymity
of a city face*

LONG AGO SUMMERS

memories
of early days and Iowa
sweet cousins
and corn

ON THE ROAD HOME

BRAZEN BIRD

so bold
to snatch
dropped French
fries beside a
young boy's feet

COOKING LESSON #1

Grandma's secret
to sliced cucumbers
crisp and paper thin
you salt and sugar
every piece
then add your
vinegar and oil

tedious and
time-consuming, yes
but pray
for your family
while slicing
they'll be blessed
with every bite

WEDDING DATE

In a cornfield-surrounded
cemetery Anna and Eugene
Sullivan were laid to rest

marble headstone
praying hands
eulogy of dates

marriage September 11, 1940
deaths 1998 and 2000

maiden daughter's
unused memorial beside them

she must have done this
this tribute to their life

and truest wedding

ON THE ROAD HOME

Happy Anniversary,
Anna and Eugene

sixty-eight years ago today

ON THE ROAD HOME

ANCIENT DWELLING

they still live you know
ancestors beloved

you hear them in quiet of
life's murmur
in cool green of
river shade
atop sunlit mesas
juniper scent baking into skin
within kiva walls
Spirit center

they tell of
caves in canyon walls
scraping scraping
obsidian tools and basalt
autumn air filled with aroma
of ground corn, baking bread

ON THE ROAD HOME

you hear
loud thumps reverberate
stone ax meets heavy beam
mano meets matate
children laugh, dogs bark

they tell of
grief and worship
death and conception
cycles of change and
continuity

you hear no
distinction between
God and government
everything is Spirit
and Spirit is everything

they pass on
knowledge, the Spirit line
like cobble rock
rounded by water
carried by the stream

ON THE ROAD HOME

SHALL I WRITE THIS?

with bare foot
I straighten the hand-
woven rug, denim on a
hard wood floor, watch
three-inch tassel threads
wave as they smoothly
slide, and I wonder
is this something to write,
would Stevenson or Kooser
or Billy Collins
pause at such a moment
and ponder the
worth of the words?

LOST LOVE

hop away
  little rabbit
I expect no
  less of you

fear clasps
  your heart
unable to
  trust

our friendship
  not meant
    to be

ON THE ROAD HOME

READING ROBERT PENN WARREN

I study golden leaves
more closely
notice specks of brown

brown the color
of mulch and forest floor
gold the color of flame

fire and rot . . . fire and rot
surely Mr. Penn Warren would
record the metaphor

aging life on a fall day

ON THE ROAD HOME

CARL AND I

I read Carl Sandburg
and wonder, are we related?
free spirits, tender souls
full of northern prairie
sun and sky

color words
red heart silver moon
blue rain
tint our
bond of life

wanderer, comrade
fellow dreamer
paint my fog
with cat's feet

Swedish American
me too
hobo heart
me too

OCTOBER SONG

russet leaves
fall like raindrops
rustle turns to
shimmer turns
to song

father wind
blows his
life breath

ON THE ROAD HOME

BRAIN FOG

like a cat
curled
napping

ON THE ROAD HOME

SHENANDOAH SPLENDOR

through woods aflutter
with wildflowers
fields tall with
tasseled corn
beside barns
and cow smells

horse-drawn rigs
clip-clop
clip-clop

between two strong arms
reaching toward the sea
in the heart of the Valley
dwell the denizens of Mole Hill

demurely dressed
heads covered
heads bowed

ON THE ROAD HOME

farm's bounty
elegant dishes
gingham cloth

feast for the flesh
feast for the eyes

feast for the soul

SHENANDOAH SPLENDOR, PART TWO

Mennonite women
make multiple
stitches,
smiling

THE ANNA TO SANTA FE TRAIL, A TRAVEL JOURNAL

December 1

Left my nest in Anna's forested hills and headed west – "on the road again" to Santa Fe. A myriad of scenes passed in peripheral vision as I traveled down Interstate 57, new sights stirring my heart. Is it the leaving or the going, or a combination of both that inspires me so to travel?

December 1st and new grass is spring-green in Alexander County's soggy bottomland, over the river and onto Missouri's Highway 60. Savored the sights of cotton fields, scenic waterways, and Ozark mountain majesties. Stepped off beaten path at Low Wassie to get out of car, feel the fresh air on my face, and ponder waking and working here.

Toppled-over barns, yards filled with a lifetime's collection of "things that may be useful some day," surrounded and secluded by high hills and nature in its wildest form. Picked sprigs of bittersweet growing along a rustic fence, hand-hewn by some long-ago farmer, and wound it into a bouquet for my dashboard.

December 2

Morning in Monett. Slept well, ready for another day driving. From East Prairie to West Plains, the span of Missouri. Daydreaming about history, a moving-picture show as I travel the miles, when Missouri was frontier Wild West, and old mining towns like Granby were considered "hot spots." How intriguing the thought of stepping back in time, to dusty dirt roads, lawlessness, and risk-filled adventure. Were there shoot-outs in these streets, bandits in bandanas, and high-speed carriage chases?

Reflected on pioneers who made this journey. Though my back gets stiff and sore from sitting, what were their aches and pains? I'm driving an air-conditioned mini-van with CD player, averaging 70 miles an hour. They plodded and bumped along as fast as an oxen team could walk, with only hat or bonnet between them and the baking sun.

December 3

Before leaving Ponca City this morning, I was beckoned by a statue of Chief Standing Bear, magnificent amid the prairie grasses, looking toward heaven, with right arm reaching upward. An informative park hostess described the local Native American history, the Kaw, Osage, Pawnee, Ponca, Otoe, and Tonkawa tribes, nomadic warriors who ultimately followed the Trail of Tears.

I felt compelled to walk the pathway, to stand before the statue, and record this poignant quote, "My hand is not the color of yours, but if I pierce it, I shall feel pain. If you pierce your hand, you also feel pain. The blood that will flow from mine will be the same color as yours. I am a man. The same God made us both." Chief Standing Bear recognized our brotherhood, even after experiencing the brutal Trail of Tears. What a legacy of forgiveness to leave for his people.

U.S. Highway 60 joins U.S. 64 just past Pond Creek, then on through Nash, Jet, and Cherokee. During long miles of isolated driving, I try to "paint" the scenery with words. Red earth wears a carpet of sage green, ragged ravines snake out of sight, yucca spikes dot distant plains, twisted cottonwoods cling to thirsty arroyos, abandoned houses with thick walls and small windows stare silently at passers by, and lonely windmills of weathered wood whisper to a bright blue sky.

Approaching New Mexico's border, first view of Rabbit Ears Mountain, then a few miles farther, snow-covered peaks in distant Colorado. As the land elevates, so does my anticipation of the splendor that's ahead. There's such a stirring in my soul, a swelling of gratitude for God's wondrous blessings. I thank Him with all my heart for this moment in time and space.

Into the Sangre de Christo foothills, the "Blood of Christ" mountains that form the backdrop of

Santa Fe, or as translated, the "City of Holy Faith." I am overwhelmed with a sense of purpose, a grand design. This rugged beauty proclaims the magnitude of creation, the "bigness" of God. Truly, truly, this is holy ground.

December 4

Woke this morning to heavy snow. Won't be going anywhere for awhile. Spent the night at Ron's ranch, sleeping in the foreman's quarters (corner of horse stable). Unpacked and reorganized, I nestled right in. Mountain views from both windows, juniper and pinon in the foreground, the Sangre de Christos stretching tall and mightily in the distance.

December 8

Finally made it into Santa Fe. Couldn't wait any longer for a laundromat. Sitting in van with warm New Mexican sun shining through window, it occurs to me, this is it. This is what I drove 1,200 miles to do, sit in van with journal in hand, waiting for clothes to wash. My destination is in the mundane after all; my contentment is in rest. The beauty around me wraps my world with His presence. I've arrived.